THE
YALE SERIES OF YOUNGER POETS

WHITE APRIL

AMS PRESS
NEW YORK

White April

HAROLD VINAL

NEW HAVEN · YALE UNIVERSITY PRESS

LONDON · HUMPHREY MILFORD · OXFORD UNIVERSITY PRESS

MDCCCCXXII

PS
3543
I 57
W5
1971

Reprinted with permission of Yale University Press
From the edition of 1922, New Haven
First AMS EDITION published 1971
Manufactured in the United States of America

International Standard Book Number:
  Complete Set: 0-404-53800-2
  Volume II: 0-404-53811-8

Library of Congress Card Catalog Book Number: 78-144718

AMS PRESS, INC.
NEW YORK, N.Y. 10003

ACKNOWLEDGMENTS.

THE Author wishes to thank the editors of *Poetry, Contemporary Verse, The Sonnet, The Atlantic Monthly, The Liberator, The Bookman, The Lyric, The Pagan, Pearson's, Tempo, The Grinnell Review, Everybody's, New Numbers, The Springfield Republican,* and *The Parisienne* for the privilege of reprinting many of the following poems.

TO MOTHER

CONTENTS.

9

PART I.
GOLDEN WINDOWS.

MY OWN.

O I must answer to a name
   And live upon a certain street,
And stairs within a dingy house
   Must bear the burden of my feet.

Still, when the night is dim and sweet,
   In dreams I roam the silent hills,
Where aisles of shadow, vague with light,
   Are petalled soft with daffodils.

I foot it through the silver dark,
   I shout aloud to field and tree
And all this gipsy heart of me
   Is longing, longing to be free.

O I must answer to a name
   And live upon a certain street,
But who shall take my dreams from me
   Or keep my life from being sweet?

CANDLE.

I WILL light my candle
  Before night comes on,
A room is a dreary place
  And forlorn.

I will light the tiny flame
  So it sputter brightly,
For ghosts of lonely things
  Trouble me nightly.

I will shut my ears
  Lest I hear again
Wind crying in the hall,
  Rain on the pane.

I will light my candle
  Before night comes on,
A room is a dreary place—
  Now love has gone.

TO PERSEPHONE.

No more you weave, Persephone,
Gowns the colors of the sea.

Your ivory fingers now are still
And your grave a grassy hill.

But everywhere songs are sung
They sing of you who died so young.

And lads and lassies passing by
Place bergamot where you lie.

No more you weave, Persephone,
Gowns the colors of the sea,

Emerald, chrysoprase and blue
That looked beautiful on you.

But everywhere songs are sung
They sing of you who died so young.

WINDOW.

FROM my window I see
  Tall trees in a row,
Rhododendron and phlox,
  Spicy things that blow.

All of beauty there
  Through four little panes,
Clumps of columbine
  Wet with the rains.

Through my window I see
  Life pass by me—
Colin and Christopher,
  Rose and Charity.

TOKENS.

IN memory of this and that
  I'll wear a starry hood
And set a bowl upon the stoop
  And light the wood.

In memory of laughter
  I'll dance no more
But hide my gown and feathers
  Behind a dark door.

In memory of sorrow
  I'll take them out again
And put a ribbon in my hair
  And dance down a lane.

FORGOTTEN.

How can I remember
  Autumn and pain,
When trees hold dreams
  In their arms again?

How can my heart break
  Till it cries?
The joy of summer
  Has made me wise.

I can't remember
  What hurt me so—
Autumn and winter
  Were so long ago.

QUERY.

I am bound by twilight,
  I am chained by snow,
I am held a captive
  To the winds that blow.

But the careless people
  Laugh as they go by
Blind to all the wonder
  Of the earth and sky;

Deaf to all the music
  Falling over me;
Is it they are captive—
  And that I am free?

DEBORAH SPEAKS.

THE candles I keep burning
   Above the door
Are in memory of those
   Who pass no more.

Faith and Caroline,
   Rose and Margaret,
I light candles there
   Lest the heart forget.

I keep candles flaming
   Lest, when Strephon call,
I forget that they
   Ever lived at all.

LESBIA SEWING.

STITCHES over and over
   So the heart won't break,
Thrust the needle under
   For sorrow's sake.

Stitches over and over
   Till the pattern's set,
Thrust the needle under
   So the heart forget.

Stitches over and over,
   Needle hurry fast,
Till the love of beauty
   Fall from me at last.

PART II.
SONNETS FOR WEEPING.

LATE AND SOON.

I AM so near to grief I needs must weep
  For little places fair as Camelot,
For dusty inns and gardens long forgot,
They haunt me ever so I cannot sleep.
I am the slave of beauty late and soon,
Of apricots blown into silver rain,
Held close to tears by many a shining lane
Where ghostly birds call wildly to the moon.
Is there at last an ending to it all,
An end of petals blown against my face,
Can I not hide myself behind a wall
And forget beauty for a little space,
Forget all passion that I ever knew—
Old beauty gone and you and you and you?

INVOCATION.

I THOUGHT that beauty was forever dead,
  Until I saw a daffodil abloom
And two bright tulips in my garden bed
And silver spills beyond my little room.
I thought that grief would never go from me,
Yet now how wonderful are all the days,
I am no longer hurt by misery
But wild with joy and tremulous with praise.
O God, let not too many white stars fall,
Nor let your bushes bloom in one small hour,
I could not bear the beauty of it all,
For I would pause with awe before each flower
And touch each blossom with my finger-tips
And feel the wind's first sweetness on my lips.

EARTH LOVER.

OLD loveliness has such a way with me,
    That I am close to tears when petals fall
And needs must hide my face against a wall,
When autumn trees burn red with ecstasy.
For I am haunted by a hundred things
And more that I have seen in April days;
I have held stars above my head in praise,
I have worn beauty as two costly rings.
Alas, how short a state does beauty keep,
Then let me clasp it wildly to my heart
And hurt myself until I am a part
Of all its rapture, then turn back to sleep,
Remembering through all the dusty years
What sudden wonder brought me close to tears.

AFTER DUSK.

BY day no singing beauty wakes in me;
    My soul is silent as a silver dell,
Where voiceless winds speak only of farewell
And cloistered flowers dwell in secrecy.
Shaken with woe I hide against my heart
Sweetness and loveliness and meadowed rain
And swallow-beauty May has brought again;
Dream-still they lie alone, untouched, apart.
But when day undesired falls asleep,
Dreaming on hills where shaking stars look down,
I roam cool-misted vales beyond the town,
And cry my love of beauty till I weep.
The glowing trees, so faint that no one hears,
Drop veils of shadow down to hide my tears.

YEAR'S ENDING.

O I could weep my heart out, late and soon,
  For dear and lovely things I would forget:
A blur of silver spills that burned at noon,
A clump of daffodils and mignonette,
Aprils remembered that come back no more
To haunt my gardens where the tulips bloom
And banished summers flaming at my door,
When haunted moonlight streamed into my room.
At times the thought of so much loveliness
Drops from me strangely, like the end of grief,
Then suddenly I feel the wind's caress,
Or a wild tree lets fall a lyric leaf.
The thought of you drifts from an ancient spring—
And I near weep again remembering.

AUTUMN AFTERNOON.

OLD loveliness returned this afternoon
  To break my heart and make me weep aloud;
I had forgotten autumn came so soon,
With blur of golden leaf and jewelled cloud.
Here once wild, scarlet tulips used to blow
And daffodils wave lightly in the spring
And lovely spicewood bushes burn and glow
And April trees spill April blossoming.
Now the last birds go winging down the air
And children's laughter and a scrap of song
Blown from a shivering pipe; Nothing lasts long,
Not even April that was once so fair.
O how it hurts to see the wild trees thinned
And spring's dear beauty falling in the wind.

EVANESCENCE.

SLOWLY I pass among the blowing flowers
  Catching my breath at their beauty as I go;
Familiar sweetness drifts across the hours,
Keen, lovely sweetness, intimate as woe.
Yet by to-morrow all the roses blown
Will be a sea of crimson on the grass,
And the naked trees will shudder at the moan
Of glowing winds that wake them as they pass.
In such wise, love will vanish as the night,
Each word of joy that you have sung to me
The years will silence with their dark delight,
And the wild soaring after ecstasy
Will be a lyric bird that dares the sky—
Only to fall to earth when storms beat by.

PITY.

O DO not pity me because I gave
  My heart when lovely April with a gust
Swept down the singing lanes like a cool wave,
And do not pity me because I thrust
Aside your love that once burned as a flame;
I was as thirsty as a windy flower
That bares its bosom to the summer shower
And to the unremembered winds that came.
Pity me most for moments yet to be
In the far years, when some day I shall turn
Toward this strong path up to our little door
And find it barred to all my ecstasy.
No sound of your warm voice the winds have borne—
Only the crying sea upon the shore.

EARTH MEMORY.

THE earth remembers many an April blown
    To lyric beauty on a lovely hill,
And many a golden hour she has known
Comes back to haunt her with old wonder still.
The earth remembers things she knew of yore,
Summers that olden lovers have forgot,
The way of silver rain upon a shore
And little towns as fair as Camelot.
The earth has moon-kissed beauty and to spare,
While I weep long for love, a thing as frail
As blue spills blown high in a sudden gale,
The space of weeping is too great to bear;
Blow by a whirl of petalled blossoming—
So I forget to weep with wondering.

PART III.
OF MARINERS.

SEA LONGING.

You who are inland born know not the pain
    Of one who longs for grey dunes and the seas
And sound of ebbing tide and windy rain
And sea-mews crying down immensities.
You who are inland born know not the urge
Of rapt tides beating passionate and wild,
Nor have you thrilled with wonder at the surge
Of drifting water, wayward as a child.
Impetuous I seek the eager sea,
Imperious for joy and wind-blown spray;
You, who are city beaten every day,
What do you know of mirth and ecstasy?
No thirsty wind has journeyed from the South—
And laid a cool, wet finger on your mouth!

EXILED.

I will remember to the very last
    The look of ships upon a quiet sea,
Each windy sail, each spar and slender mast
Must linger ever in my memory.
I will remember hills and harbor ways
And bright lagoons, though I long to forget;
Enchanted islands green as chrysoprase
And lonely nights of rose and violet.
Men who have known such splendid things as these
Can never quite forget what they have learned;
Their thoughts must always be of secret seas
Or of dim places where the moonlight burned.
Always the sound of wind moans in their ears
Or rush of waters under ghostly piers.

OF MARINERS.

You who have known the changes of the sea
    And marked the tides and watched each wistful star;
You who have known old ships, each mast and spar,
Can only know what such things mean to me.
You who have known the quiet mystery
Of lovely islands in a glowing bay,
Know what it is that haunts me night and day—
A ghost of things that will not let me be.
For they who know such things must always dream
Of wind and tide and barques that they have known,
Old schooners lying where the town lights gleam,
A tall ship sailing by at dawn alone.
They who have felt the wind upon their lips,
Their speech must always be of sea or ships.

OLD SHIPS.

What memories hang round about the spars
    Of splendid ships that come to port no more,
What dreams of moonlit seas and lovely stars,
What sound of waters on a wooden floor.
Something remembered from an ancient day
Comes back to haunt them when the evening falls,
The cry of gleaming birds from far away,
The moan of winds around their whitened walls.
Something survives to make them wistful still
Of silver harbors that they knew of yore,
Of midnight quiet by a secret hill,
Of shining lights upon a singing shore.
Perchance, a ghostly gull against the sky
Or a white sail at twilight flashing by.

LITTLE SONG.

Put a fence about my house
  It matters not to me,
If from the highest window
  I cannot watch the sea.

Scent the rooms with flowers,
  You may leave them bare
If no salty sea wind
  Wanders there.

Leave tall candles burning,
  A house can be a grave—
If it's far from water
  And a breaking wave.

THE SEA REMEMBERS.

The sea remembers things she knew of yore,
  Ships that have flowered on her lovely breast
And secret islands, silvered by a shore,
The cry of winds that mocked her with a jest.
Remembered beauty comes to haunt her still,
A ghostly sail blown by at evenfall,
A singing bird above a starry hill—
In haunted hours she remembers all.
She cannot quite forget these wistful things,
Barges that were her lovers in old days
And golden argosies with lifted wings,
And splendid schooners that sailed down her bays.
Always she dreams of masts and wooden spars
Or a tall ship that passed beneath the stars.

RUMORS.

THERE is a rumor when each ship returns
 Of ghostly harbors that it touched at dawn,
Of blue lagoons where lifted beauty burns,
Shore lines towards which its wooden spars have gone.
There is a rumor of disastrous days
And nights by quiet islands near a town,
Of wine-red hills, beyond the waterways
Where both the moon and lovely stars looked down.
Now do they dream beneath the April sky
Of olden time and golden circumstance,
Of ancient summers, ended like a dance,
And mad adventures, now a memory.
A secret flower lying on their breast
The wind dropped down upon an old, old quest.

LET ME LIE.

LET me lie in an unremembered place
 With sorrel red about me and currants swaying;
Let the cool darkness fall upon my face—
 I only want to hear waves playing.

I only ask this thing, sound of the sea,
 Clean water shifting under a granite ledge,
Spindrift flying wildly by a tree,
 The sound of the wind among the sedge.

Life must go on, to-morrow and to-morrow,
 Night following night and day following day;
Give me the one thing, Life, that I desire—
 The sound of wheeling gulls and waves at play.

PART IV.
WHITE GLAMOUR.

YOU CAME TO ME.

You came to me with darkness as a lute
   On which you played strange melodies to woo me,
You came with cymbals and wild timbrelling—
   With golden harmonies did you pursue me.

Upon a pipe of lovely shivering reeds,
   You strung your arabesques like filigrees;
The notes were kisses blown to touch my lips
   As warm as rain upon pomegranate trees.

You came to me with darkness as a lute,
   A twirl of tears to woo me and your eyes;
You brought me death and beauty, I was mute—
   Now do I hunger for you, O most wise.

THE HOUSE OF DUST.

When this, our love, at last is buried low
   Beneath the flaming streets of a dark city
And other hearts forget to scoff and pity
Our lovely dream that burned as deep as woe,
We shall arise again and gladly turn
Down these far dew-drenched vales we tread to-day
And wander where the rain-kissed boughs of May
Shed streaming perfume over starry fern.
No one will see or guess that we are there,
Who spoke their last farewell above our dust,
When our hushed voices ended all surprise,
And bitter silence for a moment thrust
Dead waves across your beauty burning fair
And petalled flowers over your sweet eyes.

35

THE NIGHTS REMEMBER.

THE nights remember lovely things they knew,
　　The words of lovers, tremulous and wise,
And kisses blown and laughter and the beauty
　　Of glowing eyes.

The nights remember hours white with wonder,
　　Lipped with red stars and strangely luminous;
Perchance, beloved, when the years have lengthened—
　　They will remember us.

UNBOUND.

SHELTER me from loving you
　　Lest it grow too great to bear,
Put a silence to my song
　　Lest it sing you everywhere.

Let me be a common hour
　　Or a careless word;
Pluck me, as you would a flower,
　　Cage me, as you would a bird.

For I praise you everywhere,
　　Shout your wonder down the street;
Bind me, so I may not dare
　　Leave you, sweet.

TALISMAN.

I SHALL remember you in years to be,
　As June's first rose or as a golden bough,
And all this beauty that we gather now
Will be a song or a dear memory.
I shall remember you as mists that blow
Across reluctant fields where no sounds are
And grief's dark night will wear a splendid star
Because of the enchanted things I know.
The peace of all your preciousness will make
Each hour of pain an hour of loveliness,
For some remembered call or faint caress
Will startle me and make my soul awake.
So I forget that woe is terrible—
Remembering that love is beautiful.

LITTLE DEATH.

YOUR love died for me
　Like rain in a hollow,
Suddenly there was no cry
　For me to follow.

All that was dear and sweet
　Last, last December,
Now is a little poem
　You can't remember.

Your love died for me
　Like mist on a bough,
Well, since I must forget—
　I will, somehow.

ROSEMARY.

For the thought of you
    I'll wind up the clock,
Sweep the floor
    And turn the lock.

For the thought of you
    I'll put on a gown,
A ribbon or two
    And go to town.

For the thought of you
    I'll talk to strange folk
And smile merrily—
    Though my heart's broke.

MOONLIGHT MAGIC.

Moonlight is magic when a day is gone
    For shivering silver hangs upon each flower;
Here where old lovers wandered once forlorn
The trees are blown to beauty in an hour.
Flowers and moonlight, these shall ever dwell
A part of beauty on each secret hill,
And whispered words that lovers dared not tell,
Will be the birth of many a daffodil.
Nor shall there be an ending to it all
For always music shall drift down the air
And shining petals tremble by a wall
And olden loveliness pass unaware.
We, who wear moonlight now like flower and grass,
In later years will bring new things to pass.

VISION.

I PUT my dream away,
  My dream of you;
A lonely little dream
  Of star and dew.

Now you can only see
  Wild April skies
When you look deep into
  My sober eyes.

So sorrowfully sad
  Their look shall be—
Your heart will never guess
  What made them see.

SONG OF YOUNG LOVE.

I MADE my love a palanquin
  From wood of Lebanon,
The seats were all of purple
  And ivory from the dawn,
For she who was to ride it
  Was fair to look upon.

I made my love a palanquin,
  Inlaid with filigrees,
The cushions were of river blue
  And color from the seas,
And there were slaves to bear it
  Dark as pomegranate trees.

I made my love a palanquin,
  The ceiling overhead
Was silver and wild olive
  And ebony and red—
I did not dream that it would be
  A place for young love dead.

PART V.
OVERTONES.

BURIED.

DEEPER far than dead men lie
   Have I buried thoughts of you
Underneath cool grasses
   And a night-green yew.

Never shall the starlings wake
   Things that lie so deep;
Never shall the sunlight stir
   Thoughts asleep.

Deeper far then dead men lie,
   Shaded and withdrawn,
I have buried thoughts of you
   From another dawn.

GLIMPSES.

I SAW a star flame in the sky,
   I heard a wild bird sing
And down where all the forest stirred
   Another answering.

All suddenly I felt the gleam
   That made my faith revive—
Ah God, it takes such simple things
   To keep the soul alive.

PASTORAL.

THE air is thin and sweet
　　With sounds I do not hear,
Somewhere beauty blows
　　As it does each year.

Somewhere laughter calls
　　Down a country lane,
But I hear the shriek
　　Of a noisy train.

Somewhere lovers wait
　　For maids undoubtedly,
Wait for a word, a kiss,
　　That belong to me.

DEATH COMES.

DEATH comes in a night,
　　All that we cherish,
Beauty and laughter
　　Soon perish.

Death comes in a day—
　　House yourself well,
Colin, Beatrice,
　　Isobel.

OLD THINGS.

Songs that I have loved
  Come back to me,
One cannot forget a bird
  Or the crying sea.

Words that I have loved
  Give the heart no rest,
Always they lie like flowers
  On the breast.

Faces I have loved,
  Eyes that gave no sign,
Did the soul behind them
  Yearn as much as mine?

MUSIC TIDES.

Tides of old music what do you sing
  Out in the darkness like a bird?
Listen and I will tell to you
  The unspeakable word.

Tides of old music what do you cry
  Out where the warm stars flame?
Bend low and I will whisper you
  The unspeakable name.

45

SURETY.

Do not weep for her who lies
    In the silences,
For she knew both youth and age
    And grew tired of these.

Do not weep for she was glad
    To share the quiet earth,
Who grew weary of such things
    As joy and mirth.

Weep only for yourself
    Who pass unsatisfied—
You have much to learn from her
    Who so gladly died.

MISER.

I have seen many things,
    Too beautiful for words;
Twilights, tremulous with mist—
    Birds.

I have heard music
    That was to me
Soft as the clinging fingers
    Of the sea.

I have known many things,
    Now I am old—
I am a miser
    Counting my gold.